COMPANION
JOURNEY

Recognizing the Presence of God
in Our Journey of Life

**Dedicated to my late husband
Deacon Jim Sura**

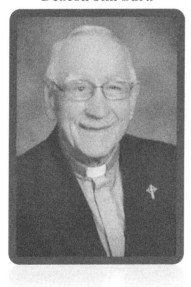

Barbara T. (Weyrens) Sura

Copyright 2022 Barbara T. (Weyrens) Sura

All rights reserved

Copy editing by Barbara's daughter Susan Lamour.

Cover Image: Barbara at Christmas Vigil. Photo by Nancy Sura.

Cover image: Barbara's granddaughter, Jordan and her husband, Parker on their *"journey together."* Photo by Susan Lamour.

Additional cover and interior layout by Susan Lamour.

ISBN: 9798366493932

CONTENTS

"Companions on Life's Journey"

♪♫ *We are companions on life's journey,*
walking hand in hand through life,
and as we travel on the path of life
We know that God is with us there
We know that God is with us there. ♫♪♫

INTRODUCTION

In your life's journey, have you ever found yourself doubting God's presence? Maybe you haven't necessarily doubted Him, but you also haven't recognized Him walking with you, carrying you – **especially** in a time of need.

Our lives are full of examples where God has been walking with us. Carrying us. Being able to recognize these moments is a gift that can make us feel more happy, more peaceful, more loved than we ever imagined.

This book shares some of my own life's journeys and recognizing God as my companion on them. Perhaps it can help to awaken an awareness of, and maybe even inspire you to share your own, journey(s) with God.

Deciding to share the following stories is one journey I never imagined for myself. I am not a writer. My husband, Jim, was a writer – not I!

Jim was an English teacher and an ordained Deacon in the Catholic Church. For more than 30 years he wrote weekly homilies and later published them in a book, "*Messages From the Heart.*" I enjoyed typing *his* manuscripts but never anticipating I would ever write a book of my own. Like Jim, I was a teacher. I taught music and art and even some quilting classes. I had no time (or desire) to write.

…But God had other plans.

After Jim's death, a voice kept telling me, "You have a story to tell. Share your journey with God as your companion. Encourage others to be companions on their own journey with God."

So, with pen in hand, I sat down, ready to tell my story. Suddenly my mind was cluttered with so many thoughts, I didn't know where to begin…

Jim and myself Many Years Into our Journey Together With God as Our Companion

QUIETING THE NOISE

Sometimes it seems we need a noise pollution ordinance for our own inner lives. Perhaps the model ordinance for us could be one used by God in Psalm 46:

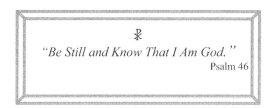

"Be Still and Know That I Am God."

Psalm 46

One of the key words in this message, "still," is a word with several meanings:

- "Still" can mean "silence."
  To be still is to be quiet, silent.

- "Still" can also mean "calm."
  "Jesus calmed the stormy sea, telling it to be still." (Mark 4:39)

- "Still" can mean "to be motionless."
  Stand still. Wait.

In one of these ways, or in all of them at once, this line from Psalm 46 can inspire help for anyone.

God never asks about our *abilities* or our *inabilities*. He only asks for our ***availability***. On the wall in my music room at school, I displayed a sign with the message, "Use the talents you possess, for the woods would be very silent if no birds sang but the best."

It has taken me more than 80 years to learn to be still enough to listen to, and genuinely hear, God speaking to me and enable me to capture in writing, some of the most significant moments in our journey together.

Two of the most significant influences God bestowed in my journey are music and my husband Jim.

Throughout this book, I share several morsels of poetic melodies that have inspired many moments. I also include some stories from Jim's life along with, "Messages From Deacon Jim," sharing quotes from his book. His deep faith, love, humor and humility through our 60$^+$year journey together have helped mold me into the person I am today.

THE JOURNEY BEGINS
My journey begins with my parents' journey

My mother, Julia, was young when her mother passed. Being the oldest child in the family, and with an overwhelmed, grieving father, she assumed the role of mother and caretaker to her 7 younger siblings. This included ensuring a proper education and guiding each of them to financially successful lives before she settled on her own vocation.

As a young adult, my mother, was a registered nurse. She tended many patients during the Great Influenza (flu) Epidemic of 1918 that killed over 500 million people world-wide.

Although she rarely shared her nursing experiences with our family, today's recent struggles with the Covid epidemic bring to light how she was a true front-line worker who survived at a time when there was no medicine to fight the "plague."

Mom was a determined woman who knew how to get things done!

My mom,
Julianna Janett (Frank) Weyrens

My dad,
Peter Matthew Weyrens

Following in his father's footsteps, my father, Peter, graduated from Teacher's College in 1912 and began teaching English and history/social studies in a small town near St. Cloud, Minnesota. He was also a member of the college football team. His love for sports led him to being a sports editor in later years.

After only a couple years of teaching, our country found itself in the midst of WWI and my dad found himself enlisting in the army. Stationed in Paris, he and several other servicemen began the army newspaper, "The Stars and Stripes."

Here he discovered his love for journalism. He traded in his teaching career and remained in newspaper business the rest of his life.

This is a great example of God's leading - even when we seem unaware of His presence.

"The Plans He Has for Us"

♪♫ Our God has plans for us.
We do not know where He is leading.
He will always keep us safe. ♫♪♫

1911 St. Cloud State College Football Team
My father is on the far left, 2nd row from the back

My parents were married in 1923 in St. Cloud, Minnesota. They moved into a new home that my father had built. As was the custom those days, my mother gave up her career as a nurse and stayed home to start and care for their growing family while my father became a very successful and respected newspaper editor.

In 1935 amidst the end of the great depression, my father moved his family with 6 kids to the small town of Park Rapids, MN to follow his dream of publishing his own newspaper. He edited and published two papers, "The Hubbard County Journal" and the "Park Rapids Enterprise."

Economically, this was an extremely difficult time to be starting a new business. As a result, six years and two more children later, he moved the family, once again, to Grand Rapids, MN to be the editor of the "Grand Rapids Independent." In a short time, he and his publisher made the decision to consolidate with the larger newspaper, the "Grand Rapids Herald Review." Here he became a notable sports editor for the Herald and a correspondent for the Duluth News Tribune.

Upon his death, a young colleague of his (Ken Hickman) had this to say:

> *"Pete Weyrens, a retired newsman was of the old school. How that typewriter would shake and jump when he pounded it. Easy-going, completely un-flappable at work, he gladly shared a lifetime of journalistic experience and wisdom with me when all I knew was what they taught us at the U. Pete had shortcuts and better ways of doing many of the things I had learned painstakingly. He was so nice and friendly that people told him things they probably never intended to reveal. Pete was a good newspaperman, a loving husband and father for a large family and a devout churchman."*

"Devout Churchman" is a key descriptor. My father and mother included God in their life and marriage and recognized His constant presence with them.

I tell this story because it reveals to us how God is always there with us through the good times and the bad during this Journey of Life and if we don't recognize His presence, our struggles can be even more difficult.

My parents, Peter and Julia Weyrens

"When You're Weary"

♪♫ When you're weary and find life burdensome,
Come to me I will refresh you
Your soul will find rest
And your burden will feel less. ♫♪♫

THE GOOD OLD DAYS

So often we speak of the "good old days;" but the "good old days" weren't always so rosy. I was born in 1936, near the end of the depression.

After the depression, the country went into a recession and 5 years later WWII was upon us. Pearl Harbor was bombed. We were practicing black out drills in the evening in our homes (just in case). Staples like gas, coffee and sugar were rationed and each family had a ration book.

I was too young to understand or even remember much of what was going on in the world. There were no televisions or social media to spread the news in real time.

Where was God in these "good old days?" In our home we spent time praying together in the evening as a family. We felt safe. I realize now it was the family praying together that made us feel this safety.

Often on Sunday evenings we listened to Fulton Sheen on the radio. One of his favorite sayings was, "The family that prays together, stays together."

After the supper meal, we would all kneel by our chairs around the dining room table and say the rosary together. Even if we had friends of another faith over for dinner, which we often did, they would kneel down with us never questioning it.

"God, I Know You are With Me"

♪♬ *God, I know you are with me*
You are always by my side
You guide me on my path, and you lead me in all of
your ways. ♬♪♬

Years later, my brother Jack's friend, Dick Randall, explained he so admired our family's faith that shortly after graduation, he became Catholic, married a Catholic girl, and chose my brother Jack to be Godfather for their son, Mark.

Jack was a lawyer who eventually became a judge. He deeply believed in the potential quality of human beings and loved hearing stories, especially of young people, who straightened out their lives after incarceration.

Notably, Jack wore a grey robe when he held court, rather than the traditional black, "Because," he explained, "Everything is not always black or white, there are many grey areas that God can lead us through if we open our hearts to Him."

The Late Judge John "Jack" Weyrens
The "Compassionate Judge"

✝ A MESSAGE FROM DEACON JIM:

"How much more beautiful the world will be when everyone hears and believes; when self-discipline prevails, and we will all feel proud of everything we do. Then, love for all of God's gifts will be the way of life. This is wisdom. It produces health to mind and body. Until everyone comes into this fold, however, you and I can listen with our heart to his gentle voice and enjoy a lifetime of peace... Even in the midst of troubles."

My parents had 8 children. I was the 7th. I thought it was large family… until I met my husband, Jim, who was the 12th of 13 children!

My family, Park Rapids, MN about 1938
Middle L-R: Alice, Margaret, Elizabeth ● Front L-R: Jack, Pete holding Jim, Barb

My four older sisters were out of high school while I was still in grade school. We didn't develop a close relationship until years later. My brothers and sisters and I were all encouraged to play the piano as well as some other band instrument.

Two of my sisters, Marian and Alice, were very talented pianists. When company would come to visit, a piano recital by both was always on the agenda. I would watch in awe as Marion's fingers would "fly" on the keyboard whenever she would play *"The Flight of the Bumblebee!"* I dreamed I could one day play so giftedly.

I never achieved their level to play and thus, never deemed myself good enough to offer my "meager" musical capabilities to anyone.

Years later, after I was married, I timidly let someone in church know I could maybe play the organ in a pinch…

This small offer grew into a lifetime of music being an integral part of my life. Because I didn't play as well as my sisters, I wasn't recognizing the ability I did have was a gift from God that He had given to me to share. It was God who put this musical desire in my heart and in so doing, this shy, introverted young girl pursued an enjoyable music career.

I have since become familiar with a prayer from St. Frances deSales explaining, "Don't waste your time dreaming of being or trying to be someone else. Work and pray at being yourself. Be who you are, where you are."

In school I learned to play the Oboe because the school owned the instrument, so my parents didn't have to buy one. I became quite good and was even awarded the honor of first chair in my college orchestra…But I also really wanted to be a part of the marching band…You don't use an oboe in a marching band! So, I joined the drum corps and learned to play the Tenor Drum! I loved learning a new routine every week to perform at half-time of the college football games.

Years later, I taught beginning students how to play their various musical instruments. In the fall, I would take them outside to march up and down the main street in Effie, MN (where our middle school was located).

Marching Band was in my blood!

In the 1982-83 school year, some temporary faculty changes, gave me the opportunity to direct the high school band in Bigfork, MN. That fall I took the band outside to march and learn a routine for half-time of the homecoming football game. They'd never done that before and the did an awesome job!

Two months later I took the band to Duluth to march in "The Christmas City of the North" parade. I had secretly dreamed of directing a high school marching band, and even though it was only for one year, God answered my desire without my asking. He truly knows our every wish.

Bigfork High School Band – 1982-83

"He Knows our Every Wish"

♪♫ *God knows our every wish*
He knows which ones he'll answer
He sends out His spirit
And His spirit sends us forth. ♫♪♫

Jim and Barb Sura
August 9, 1958

MARRIED LIFE AND FAMILY

On August 9, 1958 Jim and I were married at St. Joseph's church in Grand Rapids, Minnesota. Jim was teaching and coaching football in Sandstone, MN. This is where we started our life and family together. At the time, I was a stay-at-home mom.

Eight years into our married life, we were having dinner in our home with our parish priest and an Oblate priest who was the chaplain at the Federal Prison in Sandstone.

During dinner, Jim received a phone call from the assistant superintendent of the Grand Rapids school district. After the call, Jim relayed the message, "They've asked me to teach English in Bigfork. What do you know about Bigfork?"

I said, "I don't know much but I do know that there is no Catholic church, and I won't live in a town without a Catholic church."

The Oblate Priest at our dinner table exclaimed, "Yes, there is! The Oblates just built one there 2 years ago!" So, we packed our things and headed north to Bigfork, Minnesota. We raised our 4 children in Bigfork. It was a fun but sheltered life.

Our Family in Bigfork in the Late 1970's
Back L-R: Dave, Jim, Me ● Front L-R: Mike, Sharon, Suesie

I began teaching full-time after all our children were in school. Our small town had one school with the entire Kindergarten through 12th grade. Every day, we would all go to school together in the morning and come home together in the afternoon, unless there was some kind of practice which Jim or I any of our children were a part of.

Jim coached the boys in football and track, and I taught the girls how to play musical instruments as well as to sing and act in school performances.

On weekends we were also together participating, one way or another, at the Sunday Liturgy. The boys became altar servers, and the girls became cantors and lectors. We were all very active in church activities and the kids never complained (at least not to us). In later years, Jim studied for, and became, an Ordained Deacon in the Catholic Church.

We had 15 acres of land, and the kids were always outside with the neighbors, building tree forts or playing some kind of game and of course, snowmobiling in the winter. Hunting and fishing was a favorite past time especially for the boys and once they learned to drive they were often driving the 40 miles to Grand Rapids to have some fun with their cousins.

Being a close-knit family in a small community, it was probably easier for our kids to follow the faith path we were leading them on by example. Each of them grew up to be truly loving Christians who were very sensitive to others' needs.

In high school, our children attended TEC (Teens Encounter Christ) weekend retreats in International Falls. It was truly a wonderful faith-filled awakening weekend for each of them.

The girls became very involved with the TEC program, as did I. We made many trips to "the Falls" for TEC prayer meetings. It was a wonderful experience because it helped them delve into their faith. It was a great bible reading and learning experience for each of us in our own way… Suddenly the stories in the bible would come alive as we placed ourselves in them.

The TEC weekends placed a lot of emphasis on confession. As we prepared for confession, we spent time talking about forgiveness, forgiving ourselves and forgiving others. We would read the story of the Prodigal Son and then read a modern version to help them place themselves in the place of being forgiven:

The story is about a young man on a train:

> A young man was returning home after being gone for several years. Sitting by himself and looking quite troubled, an older gentleman asked if he could sit with him. "Where are you going?" he asked the young man. "I am going home to my father and mother - if they still want me. I have been gone for several years and I have done some things I'm not proud of."

> He continued, "I sent them a letter telling them I would like to come back home and offered: 'If you will be forgiving enough to welcome me home, please tie a white rag on the tree by the depot. If there is no rag on the tree, I will simply stay on the train and travel on.'"

> Just then, the conductor announced the young man's hometown and, "Next stop!"

> The young man was afraid to look. Then tears filled his eyes when he heard the older gentleman and many others exclaim, "Look! that tree by the depot! It is covered with white ribbons!"

In our own lives, we simply need to enter the "Reconciliation Room" and when our time down here is over, all the trees in heaven will be covered with white ribbons waiting to welcome us home.

After 32 years in Bigfork, the school district transferred me to Grand Rapids to teach. At the same time, the bishop transferred Jim to St. Joseph's, (where we made our wedding vows so many years earlier) to be the deacon there.

When we moved to Grand Rapids, Jim stated: "I had her in the desert for 40 years and now I have brought her back to the promised land."

During those 40 years there were monumental changes in the way we practiced our Catholic Faith. We found ourselves immersed in Vatican II. Suddenly:

- The altar was turned around and the priest faced the people.
- Mass was being prayed in our native language.
- We were responding with word and song!
- Lay people were allowed in the sanctuary to proclaim the readings of the day.
- We were forming committees to help make decisions on the local level that previously, were only done by the Priest.
- We no longer had to give up eating meat on Friday except during lent and we didn't have to fast from midnight if we were to receive communion at Mass.

This was an exciting time and as young Catholics; Jim and I embraced the changes and became very involved in the leadership of our local church.

Along with all these changes however, some of the traditions that were unique to our Catholic Faith were being put on the back burner so we could become more ecumenical.

As I look back on it, the greatest oversight (at least in my eyes) was the lack of emphasis on the Sacrament of Reconciliation: We no longer had to fast from midnight in order to receive Communion - which was the great miracle of the liturgy - and in so doing, people also became lax about confessing their sins to the priest!

Children still made their first communion and first confession around the age of 7 or 8. They were and still are very special sacraments; but somehow the act of confessing your sins to the priest once a month or so wasn't emphasized as it had been before. A good act of contrition would allow you to receive the body and blood of Christ which was still the highlight of the liturgy.

I admit I was as guilty as other Catechists in encouraging communion without confession unless you had committed a serious sin!

It wasn't until years later when I read a book written by Father Slavko Barbaric of Medjugorje: *"Give Me Your Wounded Heart: Confession Why? and How?"* that I truly began to understand why we need confession. One who is physically sick needs medicine and healing. One who is spiritually sick also needs healing which is found in the sacrament of Reconciliation.

Confession brings healing and health to our wounded hearts. In a good confession we not only confess the sins we have committed, but also, and most importantly, the good deeds we have left undone. In a good confession we find a deep trusting relationship with a caring priest who listens in the strictest confidence to our problems: *In what we have done and what we have failed to do.*

"Therefore," Fr. Barbaric states, "In confession there is a real meeting between man and the divine. It is made possible through a deep sharing and trust between the penitent and the priest."

Fr. Slavko died on November 24, 2000, on Mt. Lrizevac (Cross Mountain) in Medjugorje, after having prayed the Way of the Cross with the parishioners. He was 54 years old.

Mt. Lrizevac (Cross Moutain) Medjugorie

> ☧
> *"Come to me all you who are weary*
> *and find life burdensome…*
> *…For my yoke is easy and my burden light."*
> Matthew 11:28

MESSAGE FROM DEACON JIM:

"Forgiveness of Oneself and Others"

"Take some quality time each morning before beginning your day to become aware of your feelings toward those you expect to touch this day. Ask yourself, "How does Jesus feel about these people and how would he treat them if He were in my shoes?" Then raise your degrees of love for yourself and go to work. You will be more like Jesus than you were yesterday."

"He Loves us and Forgives Us"

♪♫ *We know our God's forgiving*
We know he's loving too
He welcomes us with open arms
With arms so strong and gentle
With arms so soft and gentle
He loves us and forgives us. ♫♪♫

Prior to Vatican II, the only bible in the house was the large family bible that held important family dates: baptisms, sacraments, marriages, etc.

We seldom opened it up to read, we were told we might interpret it the wrong way. Now, suddenly, we all had our own bibles, and we were writing in them and taking notes as we read passages together.

At the same time, Jim was studying for the Diaconate. I would study along with him. We had some wonderful bible study discussions with others in the program. A whole new understanding of our Catholic Faith had opened to us. God truly became the Center of Our Life.

"God, I'll Keep You in My Sight"

♪♫ God, I'll keep you in my sight,
I'll praise you morn and night,
I am here to serve you, I am here to love you
Keep me safe this day.
Keep me safe this night. ♫♪♫

CROSSES AND TRAUMAS

When we reflect on our own lives, it seems the traumas, where God so obviously carries us, are the times we remember most vividly; because that's where we grow and mature spiritually. Dr. Tom Dooley, who died of cancer at the age of 34, wrote from his death bed, "How do people endure anything on earth if they do not have God?"

I was 34 years old. The pain in my side had been bothering me for several days when I finally decided to go to the Doctor. After doing some blood tests, he sent me to a surgeon in Hibbing.

I was fortunate enough to have a sister living in Hibbing. She graciously offered to watch my children while I was in the hospital.

Putting all my faith and trust in the Doctors, I signed the necessary papers, hugged my children and husband and went into the hospital for the exploratory surgery. That was the last I remembered for several days.

I remember drifting in and out of a drug induced sleep. Everything was white around me and unfamiliar. I thought I saw a priest wearing white with a purple stole around his neck moving from bed to bed…Praying. Then I heard people crying and I thought, "He's coming for me next." Then I drifted back to sleep.

In the intensive care unit, the surgeon explained what they had done but nothing registered. I wasn't fully conscious. Later, when I woke in a regular hospital room, a woman from a colostomy support group came to talk to me…

I was dumbfounded! I was not in control of what was happening to me. God was totally in charge. "Be Still and Know That I Am God" became my daily prayer.

Over the next three years complications brought 5 more major surgeries at the University of Minnesota Hospital.

Through all the pain, I grew spiritually as did Jim, who was now fulfilling the role of both mother and father AND sole bread winner for our entire family. I acknowledged that, "Pain is inevitable, but misery is optional!" I also understood that God never gives us more then we can handle, and He gives us all we need to endure if we lean on Him with trust.

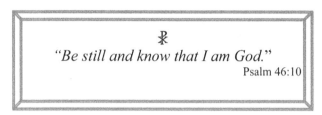

"Be still and know that I am God."

Psalm 46:10

Shortly after getting back on my feet, 3 of our 4 children were diagnosed with Scoliosis (curvature of the spine).

Our oldest son, Mike, was mostly full-grown when he was diagnosed so he could not benefit from a brace. Today the curvature still causes discomfort.

Our oldest daughter, Sharon, who was eight at the time, had the worst curvature: an "S" shape from the top to the bottom of her spine. For 8 years, she wore a full-length "Milwaukee" brace 23 hours a day. Our youngest daughter, Suesie, wore a half-length "Pelvic" Brace for 5 years, 23 hours a day.

As the girls grew, their braces needed to be replaced with larger ones. The bills were piling up. All our kids were not in school…It was time for this "stay at home" mom to go work!

Where was my husband, Jim during this time? He was carrying us – ALL of us - with prayer and compassion, and with humor. He never failed to find something to laugh about and was always able to see and help us feel the sunshine, even when the clouds hung low.

A quote from *God's Little Devotional Book for Women*, reads:

"At times, some situations in our lives are so desperate and our pain so deep, we can only muster 9-1-1 prayers to God. These are called "SOS" prayers and they often use the same words, "God, I need help!"

"God hears each one. He knows our name and every detail of the situation. Like a heavenly dispatcher, He will send precisely who and what is needed to assist us."

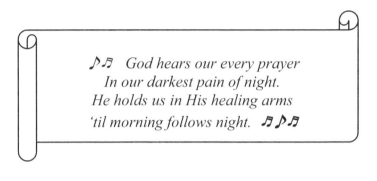

♪♫ *God hears our every prayer*
In our darkest pain of night.
He holds us in His healing arms
'til morning follows night. ♫♪♫

When Jim was accepted into the Diaconate program, it meant 4 years of study for both of us because even though only the husband is ordained, the wife must go through all the training and schooling with him to fully understand his ministry.

We went to Duluth one weekend each month. Part of the time was spent in Spiritual Direction where we were introduced to Spiritual Journaling. It was a wonderful growth experience in my religious journey. After a time, however, I became involved in other aspects of my faith and stopped journaling.

In December 1980, I registered for an Advent Retreat at the McCabe Center in Duluth. I decided to start journaling again. It had been good for me, and I was excited to get back into it. With my new notebook safely packed, my friend and I headed to Duluth.

When we reached the Retreat Center, the Sister informed us there was a blizzard coming and there would only be three people on the retreat! Normally, such a small turnout would result in cancellation. I must have looked like I really needed it, because they decided to move ahead with it.

After the Friday evening meal, we gathered in the living room where Sister asked, "Have any of you heard of Spiritual Journaling? "That's what we're going to focus on this week-end." …What a coincidence!

She taught us something excitingly new about journaling: "God often speaks to us in our dreams. If you feel He has spoken to you in a dream, go to your journal and write from the back. At some point the conscious (your regular journaling) and unconscious (journaling about your dream) meet."

After some discussion, our director said we would be doing the healing of memories prayer. I thought, "not that again!" I had been at McCabe several years before and carried away a terrible memory:

> During the prayer, we were told to lay down on the floor and relax while someone read it. The gal who came with me to the retreat was lying next to me on the floor and early in the prayer, she fell asleep and began to snore very loudly! I kept nudging her to wake her up but I had a charm bracelet on that made as much noise as her snoring! Needless to say, I got nothing out of the prayer and hoped I never had to go through that again.

This time, thankfully, no one fell asleep. After the prayer, we visited a while went off on our own. I sat by the fire for a while and then went to bed.

About three o'clock in the morning I startled awake, sitting straight up in my bed, I was grasping my pillow in my arms and sobbing. My dream unfolded before my eyes:

I was holding my mother in my arms as she was dying. We were expressing our love for each other…and then in the next instance, I undeniably felt someone holding on to me. I touched my shoulder to see who was there and felt nothing but a vivid, glowing peace flow warmly through me.

It was six years to the day of my mothers' passing when she and I finally shared this beautiful goodbye… My sisters were with her when she passed but didn't call me until morning. When I arrived at the hospital, she had already passed away.

I heavily missed saying a final goodbye to mom. My dream was a gift... A glorious gift… Can you imagine? 6 years later, an opportunity to see and feel and talk and to cry with my mother!

This time, the Healing of Memories prayer had touched me deeply. The whole experience showed me that God leads us where he wants us and when He knows we're ready to be there.

"Tears"

♪♫   *Our tears can bring us sadness or joy*
Our loving Lord will guide them
But when in sadness they begin to fall
His loving spirit will touch them
His loving spirit will change them.
He turns our sadness to joy. ♫♪♫

The phone call came at 11:00 A.M. . . .

My sister, Marion, was working at the hospital in Grand Rapids and she explained, "Mike has been in a terrible accident. He's still alive. Get here as quick as you can!"

Arriving at the hospital in record time, we found Fr. Jerry Weiss and my sister sitting quietly with Mike. We prayed together then left the room. The doctor came to us in the waiting room and said, "You must have great connections with God. Your son is going to live but not because of anything I did."

Mike was attending junior college in Grand Rapids and had just picked up two friends on their way to morning class. While crossing a set of unmarked railroad tracks, they were hit by a train! All three were thrown from the vehicle in one lifeless heap.

There were more friends in another car and. One friend ran to the bodies while another cried, "Stay back, they're all dead!" Hysterically, he pulled Mike out from the other bodies and began giving him mouth to mouth resuscitation, breathing life back into his body, keeping him alive until the ambulance arrived.

Despite a punctured lung and a collapsed lung, and many fractures, Mike did indeed survive. For this, we, are obviously so very grateful, but being the driver in an accident where his two friends did not survive, weighs heavy on him so many years later.

Seeing someone we love suffer is more painful than if we had to bear it ourselves. What got me through this pain was envisioning Jesus' mother Mary watching her son tortured and crucified! If we can be still, quietly praying and relying on God's grace, much good can come even in unbearable times.

Several years later, we received another devastating phone call:

Our second son, Dave, was working in a tire shop, repairing a large truck tire when it exploded on him!

As the tire blew, he instinctively brought his arm up, saving his head from a deadly blow, but shattering the arm, and crushing his nose into the front part of his brain!

Dave had impressive strength in his arms from lifting weights, and although his arm was shattered, it was able to break the force of the tire enough to save his life. His elbow was gone, his shoulder ans right hand were shattered.

When we arrived at the hospital in Duluth 3 hours later, he was still in surgery. When he came out of surgery, he was unrecognizable. He had a plate in the front part of his brain and his nose was gone.

His right eye was swollen shut and so bruised it was questionable if he would ever see with it again. …Interestingly, this ended up being the one eye he *would* see with because the injury to the right side of the brain had caused blindness in the left eye.

Months later, after several neuro and plastic surgeries, we could see the healing begin, we were able to find a little humor and start to laugh again.

Once again, God carried our cross as we reflected in gratitude how any human can live through such trauma without God's embrace.

☧

"The Lord is my shepherd. There is nothing I shall want.
He guides me in right paths for his name's sake
Even though I walk in the dark valley
I fear no evil, for you are with me...."   ~ Psalm 23

"My Cross"

♪♫ *My cross is heavy Lord,*
I cannot carry it alone.
Once again, I cry for help,
Its weight feels much like stone.
You alone can help me, Lord.
You help me with my cross
Once again, I cry for help;
and once again you're there.
Praise and thank you Jesus Lord,
Praise and thanks to God our King. ♫♪♫

Tragedies and pain can strike any person.

We need to allow God to put us back together according to his design rather than trying to find all the pieces and glue ourselves together without Him.

I had been at a math conference in Minneapolis when I felt the first pinch in my back. By the time we had returned home to Bigfork, I was having trouble even getting out of the car.

For the next six weeks, I couldn't walk down the school hallway without having to stop to rest. The pain was exhaustingly increasing, and I couldn't relieve it with any medication.

I had already been registered for the National Pastoral Musicians Conference in Indianapolis, Indiana before this problem started. I decided to go, thinking I would be okay as long as I used a cane and didn't walk too much.

At the conference, I attended a healing mass. I had people praying over me and with me… but no "healing" was happening.

A week after returning from Indianapolis, I attended a women's silent retreat in Buffalo, Minnesota. I was once again prayed over at a healing mass and again, nothing changed.

After returning home from Buffalo, I had an appointment with a Neurosurgeon in Duluth. The night before the appointment, Jim and I were watching the news and then switched over to the 700 club.

Pat Robertson was praying for people with different ailments. Our skin prickled when he said, "There is a woman, her name in Barbara. She has been suffering from terrible back pain and she is being healed." Jim and I looked at each other skeptically. …"Not possible."

The show ended and I crawled upstairs to bed. (At this point, I could no longer walk up them.)

In the middle of the night, I woke and went into the bathroom. After returning to bed, I realized I had just walked down the hallway and back…WITHOUT PAIN! I had been healed!

The next morning, we decided we should still keep my appointment in Duluth and headed out. I told the doctor that I felt a little foolish for taking his time and a bit skeptical telling about him my story. He looked at me and said, "We need help from the man upstairs too!"

Being the cradle Catholic I am, I want to believe the healing was a delay from the earlier Healing Mass… It just took Pat Robertson to tell me!

God answers our prayers in his time, reminding us we are not in control. He will answer all our prayers but not always when or how we want, but He will, in His way, and at the best time.

✞ A MESSAGE FROM DEACON JIM:

"Life is a beautiful gift! How I choose to handle happenings is what I give to the world. The world grows stronger or becomes weaker from the way I feel and react to its offerings."

"We Give Thanks to God"

♪♫ *Our hearts give thanks to God above*
Our hands and voices too
You shower us with unending love
We send our thanks to you. ♫♪♫

LAUGHTER, THE BEST MEDICINE

"We don't stop laughing because we grow old, we grow old because we stop laughing."

The pricelessness of laughter is deeply evident when reading passages from my husband's book. He recounts many moments from his life where laughter really was the best medicine.

Jim was a very humble and holy man with a gift of being able to laugh at himself. As I mentioned earlier, he rarely failed to find something to laugh about and was always able to find the sunshine, even when the clouds hung low.

An ordained Deacon in the Roman Catholic Church for 30 plus years, Jim was a true example of what it means to accept who you are and with God's help make the most of it.

When Jim was a young boy (10 years old), he had a brain bleed that left him unconscious for several days. He was not expected to live.

With many prayer warriors and skilled doctors, he miraculously woke up, quite his normal self. He did, however, suffer short term memory loss that would affect him the rest of his life.

Not many people knew of Jim's memory loss or its cause. They often kidded him about being an "absent minded professor." When colleagues and friends would chide him about forgetting something he would just laugh it off!

Despite his slight "disability," Jim earned a master's degree in Counseling. He counseled troubled teens both at Thistledew Boys Correctional Facility and the high school where we both taught.

Jim will always be remembered for his infectious laugh and smile. A true gift from God.

Jim found joy in so many things. Here he is joyfully immersed in a "forest" of mallow plants at the farmer's market.

> ☧
> *"A Glad Heart lights up the face."*
> *"A cheerful glance brings joy to the heart."*
>
> Proverbs 15: 13, 30

A genuinely happy man with a truly happy heart.

"Happy the Man"

 *Happy the man who wanders with the Lord.*

Happy the man who knows how to live.

Happy the man who never seeks reward.

Giving because he loves to give.

He seeks no gold. He wants no gain.

He knows those things are all in vain.

He needs no praise, nor honor too.

His only motto, "To your own self be true."

Happy the man who learned how to pray

Happy the man who has a burning goal.

Happy the man whose service needs no pay.

This man has found his own soul.

Happy the man. Happy the man of the Lord.

~ Sebastian Temple

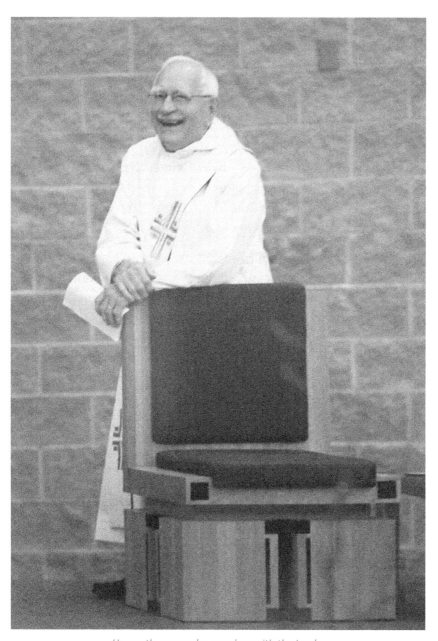

Happy the man who wanders with the Lord...

God and His presence never cease to amaze me:

I was planning a witness talk for a women's retreat and wanted to add a bit humor into it. I was married to a man who taught me to laugh at myself in good or bad times and to always find some joy in life. I wanted to share that gift in my talk.

At the same retreat, Fr. Tom Radaich, the pastor at St. Joe's at the time, was asked to give a mini talk about the Holy Spirit - just before my witness talk.

Ironically, the Lord must have "divinely intervened" because without knowing what I was about to say in my talk, Father began with several jokes and then quoted scripture, "I will go to the altar of God, the God who brings joy to my youth."

He went on to say, "The Spirit represents joy and happiness and that's so important – especially in our world and our church today where there is so much polarization and dissention going on. The ability to laugh is a sign of the spirit. This spirit brings joy and revitalizes my youth."

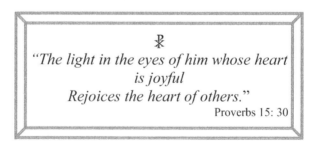

"The light in the eyes of him whose heart is joyful Rejoices the heart of others."
Proverbs 15: 30

Fr. Tom Volunteering at the "Community Café" (Local Free Meal Kitchen).

I have found in my life that when things begin to get tense, God is always there with whatever we need at the time, and if we look for it, can also find a dash of humor.

I think people often put clergy, (and spouses of clergy), on pedestals. There can be a lonely space where it almost feels impossible to just be who we are without feeling scrutinized. This really hit home when we first moved to Grand Rapids: I didn't know a lot of the people in the church community by name. I had volunteered to help a friend of mine work with St. Joe's food booth at the county fair.

At one of the planning meetings, one of the ladies was trying to coach me how to call people and talk them into working a shift or two at the fair booth. After listening to her for a while, I frustratingly said, "I think I'll just let the deacon do the calling!" She looked at me in shock and replied, "That's who you are? You're not that holy!"

I'm still working on being holy, even today; but I keep falling off that pedestal! We had some very memorable times working at the fair and serving "St. Joe's Heavenly Chicken." I loved working with my dear friend, Mary Jo, who had an infectious laugh - like my husband's. It made all the long hours joyful. Together, she and I were able to turn some possible disasters into memorable, laughable moments.

True Food Booth Story:

We had two well-known members of our church community, volunteering with the early morning food prep. After breading the last leg of the entire day's worth of chicken, we realized, in horror, they used pancake mix instead of breading mix!

We had to wash it all off and start all over again!

Father Tom with his 2 "confessors," Dr. Karges and Dr. Coy, who attempted to make "Pancake Chicken" at the fair.

Mary Jo and me in the church food booth at the Itasca County Fair

Another True Food Booth Story:

An elderly volunteer brought a large box of pies to the booth. It was heavy and cumbersome, so she set it on a small nearby stool. As she turned around, the box fell off and all of the pies fell together!

Solution? We mixed all the pies together and served, "Fruits of the Forest Cobbler" with a dollop of whip cream.

It was such a hit, the customers were asking for it the next day!

Mary Joe Peddling the
"Fruits of the Forest" Cobbler

We worked many long hours at the fair and God was present through it all. It was wonderful to see all ages of our church community volunteering and working together. It was even more wonderful to recognize and share the humor He sprinkled in here and there, making it a memorably joyful experience for all!

Mary Jo was a special gift – but not only in the food booth. She passed away as I was writing this book but her joy, even today, continues to overflow into every-day life. She taught me so much about faith and was a true prayer warrior who spent many hours daily praying for those in need, and always with a joyful heart.

Fr. Tom Socializing in the Fair Booth

> ☧
> *"A happy heart is good medicine*
> *And a cheerful mind works healing."*
> Proverbs 17

The Jolly Fair Booth Crew

There have been many lovely pictures of Jesus, painted by an array of artists imagining what He looked like.

Being a visual learner myself, I love looking at the many variations whether it be pictures depicting the Stations of the Cross or the more joyous days before he was betrayed suffered at the stations.

I often wonder, "What was the artist thinking or praying when he or she painted a particular picture?"

There is one picture of Jesus that many people may not have seen: *"Jesus Laughing."*

I think of this picture whenever I recall perhaps the most embarrassing moment of my life:

We were at a semi-formal Diocesan dinner in Duluth. I was chairman of the newly formed Diocesan Pastoral Council. I was feeling proudly important as it had scored Jim and me a seat at the head table with Bishop Anderson.

I was heading back to my seat with a plate full of spaghetti and meatballs. Just as I was passing behind Jim, he raised his hand to acknowledge someone, smacking my plate firmly into my chest. I had Spaghetti and Meatballs running literally from head to toe!

I didn't know whether to laugh or cry. I laughed. I continue to laugh today each time I retell this story. It taught me to laugh when I really wanted to cry.

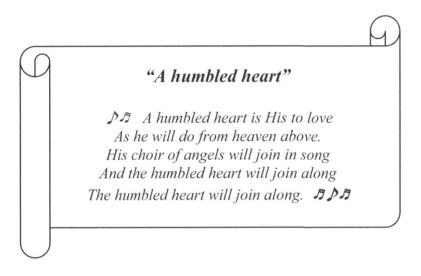

"A humbled heart"

♪♫   *A humbled heart is His to love*
As he will do from heaven above.
His choir of angels will join in song
And the humbled heart will join along
The humbled heart will join along. ♫♪♫

On a serious note, this incident taught me a great lesson in humility and reminds me of a message my husband delivered in his book: "A humbled heart is a fulfilled heart."

✝ A MESSAGE FROM DEACON JIM:

"May the humility and wisdom of Jesus open wide the door to your heart so that he may accomplish more deeply what he has come to do."

PILGRIMAGES AND MIRACLES

I have been very fortunate in my lifetime journey to visit many beautiful, holy places, here in the United States and throughout the world. God has been good to me.

Many of the places I have traveled to were not intended to be a pilgrimage but, on each trip, the Lord led me on an unexpected journey that turned it into a memorable pilgrimage where I received spiritual nourishment.

Come and journey with me as I take you on some of my memorable pilgrimages.

"Holy Ground"

♪♫ *This is Holy Ground.*
We're standing on holy ground,
for the Lord is present
and where He is…
Is holy! ♫♪♫

St. Patrick's Cathedral, New York City
February 2019

Notre Dame Cathedral, Paris, France
Gaudete Sunday, 2016

✞ A MESSAGE FROM DEACON JIM:

"Faith is a beautiful gift! How I choose to handle things that happen is what I give to the world. The world grows stronger or becomes weaker from the way I feel and react to its offerings. It takes FAITH.

Faith allows one to believe in miracles... A belief in miracles inspires a more fervent faith... Faith creates longing and a desire to draw closer... The site of a miracle becomes a point of focus... The pilgrim makes his or her way there and then, arriving, finds that faith and inspiration overflow.

We stand on Holy Ground each time we enter a Catholic Church where Jesus is present in the Tabernacle, and we witness a miracle each time the priest changes the bread and wine into the body and blood of Christ for us to partake in!

Our Lady of the Snows Catholic Church, Bigfork

It doesn't matter if Mass is being offered in a small country church in northern Minnesota or a glorious cathedral in New York City or Paris. It is a blessing and joy for our priests to consecrate the host at every mass.

He has holy hands and each time we touch his hands our hearts should leap for joy because his hands are holy!"

Father Blake Consecrating the Host at Mass

"THE BEAUTIFUL HANDS OF A PRIEST"

We need them in life's early morning. We need them again at its close. We feel their warm clasp of true friendship. We seek them when tasting life's woes. At the altar each day we behold them. And the hands of a king on his throne; Are not equal to them in their greatness; Their dignity stands all alone.

When we are tempted and wander the pathways of shame and sin, 'Tis the hand of a priest that will absolve us - not once, but again and again. And when we are taking life's partner, other hands may prepare us a feast. But the hands that will unite and bless us, are the beautiful hands of a priest.

God bless them and keep them all holy for the Host which their fingers caress. What can a poor sinner do better but ask him to guide thee and bless.

When the hour of death comes upon us, may our courage and strength be increased by seeing raised over us in blessing, the beautiful hands of a priest.

Grotto of the Redemption.
West Bend, Iowa

"On This Day O Beautiful Mother"

♪♫ *On this day O beautiful mother*
On this day we give thee our love.
Near thee, Madonna, fondly we hover,
Trusting thy gentle care to give! ♫♪♫

~ GROTTO OF THE REDEMPTION ~
West Bend, Iowa

As you approach the Grotto of the Redemption in West Bend, Iowa, you can hear Marian hymns quietly beckoning you to enter. You feel God's presence, and know you are on Holy Ground.

The Grotto is a assemblage of nine grottos depicting scenes from the life of Jesus. It contains more than 250 types of semiprecious stones from amethyst to drury quartz and a large collection of minerals and petrifications.

The Grotto of the Redemption is believed to be the largest in the world. Despite its size, it is overwhelmingly humbling as you walk along rocky paths to view each grotto.

Construction of the Grotto began in 1912 by Fr. Paul Dobberstein after recovering from a life-threatening bout of Pneumonia. As he fought for his life, he prayed to the Blessed Virgin Mary to intercede for him for the grace of good health. He promised to build a shrine in her honor if he lived.

He survived! He built his grotto in West Bend where he was the pastor of Saints Peter and Paul church.

Fr. Dobberstein was confident that when he finished, his project would speak for itself... And that it does!

It was constructed completely by hand with the help of a young man, Matt Szerensce. From the time he graduated high school through its completion 52 years later, Matt worked full-time, unbelievably placing each and every rock any mineral by hand!

Deacon Jim and I have led several pilgrimages to the Grotto. My heart continues to be humbled by its natural beauty every visit.

Grand Rapids pilgrims by the Grotto of the Redemption entrance
"Open wide the doors to Christ"

Assumption Chapel (Grasshopper Chapel)
Cold Spring, Minnesota

~ ASSUMPTION CHAPEL ~
Cold Spring, Minnesota

In 1873, Rocky Mt. Locusts (Grasshoppers) descended with a vengeance upon much of the Upper Midwest.

The grasshoppers consumed pretty much anything they came in contact with including crops, fruit, wood and even clothes! For 4 years, in the early summer, the grasshoppers hatched from eggs laid the previous year and the cycle started all over again.

The swarms of grasshoppers were unstoppable. In 1877 Minnesota Governor John Pillsbury enacted a statewide day of prayer but they didn't yield.

Fr. Leo Winter, pastor of two Stearns County congregations, recommended a petition to the Blessed Virgin Mary for relief from the grasshoppers. The congregations both agreed and in July 1877 construction began on the Assumption Chapel. The chapel was built on a hilltop overlooking Cold Spring, Minnesota as a plea to God to make the onslaught end.

Mysteriously (or miraculously), around the same time construction began, the swarms of Grasshoppers flew away. By the time the chapel was completed, and Masses began, not a single grasshopper could be found!

The grasshoppers never returned and less than 30 years later, that species had become extinct. The people had faith that Mary would intercede - and she did.

In 1894, the original chapel was destroyed by a tornado and the hilltop stood empty for decades. In 1952 a new chapel was built to replace the original chapel. Displayed prominently near the altar is the statue of the Blessed Virgin Mary from the original chapel.

Over the entrance to the chapel is a relief of Mary with 2 grasshoppers kneeling on each side. Outside surrounding the chapel are the Stations of the Cross.

As pilgrims reach the hilltop, they become absorbed in the serene chapel and outdoor stations whose simple beauty and story fills them with a calming peacefulness. They know they are on Holy Ground.

Deacon Jim led our group of pilgrims on the Way of the Cross. Because we were on ground dedicated to Mary, we said "Mary's Way of the Cross."

It was a powerful, prayerful experience. As Jim approached the 4th station (Jesus Meets His Mother), he become so overwhelmed with emotion, he began sobbing. The pilgrims, many with tear-filled eyes, were inspired to join Jim in leading the rest of the stations together.

It was the most meaningful Stations of the Cross I had ever experienced.

Grand Rapids Pilgrims in Front of the
Grasshopper Chapel

~ CAMP ST. MALO ~
Allenspark, Colorado

We were visiting our daughter, Sharon, who had recently relocated to Colorado. Together, we took a trip to Estes Park. It was not meant to be a pilgrimage, but God had a surprise for us!

On our descent, as we rounded one of the many curves and there, standing high upon a mountain ledge, was a statue of our risen Lord watching down over a beautiful stone chapel, Camp St. Malo. We knew we were on Holy Ground and stopped to pray.

Magic Morn After the Storm Camp St. Malo – Allenspark, CO

Pope John Paul II Visiting
Camp St. Malo – Allenspark, Colorado

Pope John Paul II visited the chapel at Camp St. Malo on World Youth Day in 1993 and had this to say:

"Upon arriving in Denver, I lifted up my eyes to the splendor of the Rocky Mountains, whose majesty and power recall that all our help comes from the Lord, who has made heaven and earth. 'He alone is the rock of my salvation.' " (cf. Ps. 121:1, Ps. 89:26)

"Against the splendid backdrop of the Colorado mountains, with their pure air which bestows peace and serenity on nature, the soul rises spontaneously to sing the praise of the Creator: 'O Lord, Our Lord, how glorious is your name over all the earth!' " (Psalms 8:1)

"Open My Eyes"

♪♫ Open my eyes, Lord. ~Help me see your face.
Open my eyes, Lord. ~Help me to see.
Open my ears, Lord. ~Help me hear your voice.
Open my ears, Lord. ~Help me to hear.
Open my heart, Lord. ~Help me love like you.
Open my heart, Lord. ~Help me to love. ♫♪♫

Cathedral of Santa Maria del Fiore, Florence, Italy
Displaying One of Florence's Famous Domes

~ ITALY ~
Florence, Rome, Assisi

My trip to Italy was my first pilgrimage to Europe and to Holy Cities. I was joining our Bishop at the time, Roger Schweitz and his family as well as other pilgrims from throughout the Duluth Diocese.

The only person missing was my husband, who was on a long-anticipated elk hunting trip with our sons. The opportunity for this journey to the Holy Land was so unique, I decided to go ahead and experience the unbelievable beauty on my own.

One cannot describe the beauty of the art and architecture in these cities, you really do have to see it to believe it. Books and pictures can't begin to describe it.

━━━━━━━━━━━━━

The Renaissance City of Florence, Italy is where we started our pilgrimage. We viewed famous sculptures and toured so many Cathedrals, each was more beautiful than the last. Much of the artwork depicts scenes from the life of Christ.

The sites were phenomenal! They were also seemingly endless – which was both a blessing and a hindrance as we had so many to tour, we didn't have time to absorb the grandeur of one before we were whisked away to the next. I knew that God was with us, but it was hard to focus on His deep presence in the rush.

St. Peter's Basilica - Vatican City, Italy

Sistine Chapel – Vatican City, Italy

We traveled next to Rome. Our first stop was St. Peter's square and the Basilica on Vatican Hill. The most beautiful masterpieces ever created by man are inside that Basilica.

Millions of Catholic Pilgrims visit each year to view these significant religious masterpieces such as Bernini's baldachin and cathedra architecture and Michelangelo's breathtaking *Pietà*.

Although Michelangelo insisted he was a sculptor not a painter, his masterpiece painting on the ceiling of the Sistine Chapel is indescribable. His work of genius depicts the book of genesis starting with the creation of Heaven and earth, followed by the creation of Adam and Eve, the Garden of Eden and Noah and the great flood.

Michelangelo was a devout Christian who knew the Old Testament well. The presence of God in his life so obviously shows in his ability to depict the Book of Genesis and as he continued to create masterpiece after masterpiece.

How wonderful it would have been to view the Sistine Chapel all alone in silence with only God as my companion and guide. Unfortunately, this is not possible. You need a ticket for a specific date and time; and regardless of the "reservation" there were so many people touring, it was impossible to take the time I would have liked to view this incredible masterpiece. It felt I was being challenged by God to filter out the activity around me and just feel His presence in my heart.

Pope John Paul II once commented, "Sometimes this seems more like a museum than a Cathedral." His point was so true. These artists had God-gifted talents, not only for painting and sculpting, but in designing such structures with massive domes and appendages. They truly harnessed these gifts, turning them into eternal works of art that enforce God's sustaining presence even without a formal religious service…Just like a museum!

Assisi is a well-preserved medieval village with its old stone buildings and narrow winding cobblestone walkways and streets that make you want to slow down and "smell the roses." Here is where I most significantly felt God's presence on my journey

After vigorously walking along these winding streets, we came upon the Basilica of St. Mary of the Angels.

Upon entering her massive structure, we were greeted by a quaint, humble church *within the larger church.* This is the original church that St. Francis and his followers built and where he established the Franciscan Order. The Basilica of St. Mary of the Angels was built around St. Francis' original church!

The interior of this simple church is very peaceful and welcoming as though it is inviting you to stay and pray a while.

The original chapel Where St. Francis of Assisi Lived and
began the Franciscan Order.
The Basilica of St. Mary of the Angels
Was Later Uniquely Constructed Around This Chapel

The Basilica of St. Francis is built in a hill overlooking Assisi. It the mother church of the Roman Catholic Order of Friars Minor Conventual. There are actually two churches: an upper and a lower, following the hill slope, with a crypt below them where St. Francis is interred.

The basilica was badly damaged during an earthquake in 1997. It took several years for restorations that could not have been accomplished without the artists' love of God and His presence guiding them through with compassion and love.

Upper and Lower Churches of the Basilica of St. Francis of Assisi, Italy

In remembering my pilgrimage to Italy, I cannot compare one city or cathedral to another because they each have their own grandeur and beauty. You feel God's presence in the grandest, most ornate cathedrals all the way to the humblest of grottos because in all of them you know you are on "Holy Ground."

~ IRELAND ~

There is something special and heartwarming about the Irish! Their genuine humility and simple pleasures bring a peacefulness, even to strangers.

One evening we asked our tour guide where we could go to spend some time with the "locals." He directed us to a Pubs near our hotel and assured we would have a great time.

To our surprise, the pub was filled with families with children, visiting and enjoying traditional Celtic songs from the two guitarists and a fiddler.

We were excited to have the musicians invite Jim to play the fiddle on a tune he knew. This was a most incredibly memorable evening living in the moment with the locals and God as our companion.

Mount Croagh Patrick in County Mayo, is considered the holiest mountain in Ireland. In 441 AD, St Patrick spent the 40 days of Lent praying and fasting on the mountain top as part of his effort to convert Ireland to Christianity.

Many, like this man, make the pilgrimage each year climbing on the rough, rocky path to reach the Croagh Patrick's summit.

Pilgrim Praying on the Holy Mountain of Croagh Patrick

The Cliffs of Moher is one of Ireland's most beautiful, awe-inspiring attractions. As we set out for the day's tour, we were forewarned if the foggy weather didn't lift, the Cliffs would not be visible.

It had been dreary for several days and the forecast was not promising. Incredibly, as the day progressed, the mists faded, the fog lifted, and we were able to witness the grandeur of this beautiful landscape shaped by our Creator!

It was another miracle bestowed on our journey and another teaching moment: "Be Still and Know That I Am God."

Jim and I and the Cliffs of Moher

"Morning's Mist"

♪♫ As mornings mist reveals His love
We look to him in heaven above
We thank you Lord, for this new day
We pray that in your arms we'll stay. ♫♪♫

~ AUSTRIA & SWITZERLAND ~
Where were you on 9/11?

"Kindness is a language which the deaf can hear and the blind can see;" a quote aptly penned by famous author, Mark Twain. "And," I would add, "Can be understood in any language."

In September 2001, Jim and I embarked on a journey we had dreamed of for years: Austria and Switzerland. We left home on September 6th with a return date of September 16th.

September 11, 2001. As we pulled up in front of our hotel after a beautiful day of sightseeing, our tour director stood at the front of the bus and announced, "We have some difficult news before you leave for the evening."

His tone was somber and sincere. We tensed as he continued, "Early this morning, the United States was attacked by terrorists! Our hearts go out to you. We know how you are feeling as we lived through similar attacks during World War II."

We were stunned!

Rushing to our rooms, we turned on our televisions looking for the news channel that had complete coverage (in English). Upon entering, we found notes on our beds from the hotel employees filled with so much compassion and kindness, it was overwhelming.

We were staying in the small village of Grindelwald, in the Swiss Alps. The evening after the attacks, the villagers held a special service in their quaint little chapel in the village square. The entire church, and its grounds outside was **filled** with townspeople.

At the front of the church, in front of the altar, a coffin had been placed, draped in black with a large spray of flowers in remembrance the dead. All the readings and messages were spoken in German then again in English. God's presence was so evident, we knew we were on Holy Ground.

Many of the villagers had lived through WWII and remembered sympathetically, the complete helplessness, sadness, and shock we were feeling. This was a loving act of kindness we never forgot.

"Be Still"

♪♫ Be still, I am with you,
I will hold of you in my arms.
Come and follow me,
And I will keep you safe.
Be Still my soul, be still... ♫♪♫

Small chapel in the little village of Grindelwald,
Switzerland where they held a special service the day
after the 911 attacks in the U.S.

~ MEDJUGORJE ~
Bosnia and Herzegovina (Yugoslavia)

In 1858 the Virgin Mary appeared to young Bernadette in Lourdes and again to 3 peasant children in 1913 Fatima.

In our lifetime, (1981) two boys and four girls in the small mountain village of Medjugorje, Yugoslavia (now Bosnia-Hercegovina) reported she came to them with a message of peace. These 6 "messengers" are still alive today.

Although the Catholic Church has not embraced it as a miracle, Pope John Paul II spoke several times of his belief that something very special had happened in Medjugorje.

Medjugorje is not a beautiful stunning city but rather a humble, hilly, rocky village. There streets were not paved, and we walked everywhere. We felt like true pilgrims as we were hosted in the homes of the village residents.

Remarkably, it felt like the holiest place I had visited. It seemed to me this tiny little village was comparable to where Jesus lived in his youth!

Although we were wearing walking shoes and using walking sticks, as we had been told, we still felt the pain of the rocks under our feet as we hiked to the top of Cross Mountain. As challenging as it was you could feel the presence of God in all who traveled with us.

Of all of the "Holy" places I have traveled, this is the place I would eagerly travel to again.

All the material things of our world were lost as we were hosted in this tiny village of mostly peasants. It felt like simply walking on this holy ground was a miracle.

Mary in Front of the Village Church, Medjugorje, Bosnia

*One of the Stations on the Rough and Rocky Trail
to the Top of Cross Mountain, Medjugorje*

A MIRACLE?

So, what is a miracle? If we are aware of God's presence every day of our lives, we will witness some form of miracle each day. God has been good to me on my life's pilgrimages, by making me more aware of the beauty of this world he has created.

Our world is often gentle but can also be harsh and impersonal. We can lose gentleness and fail to accept peace from the hand of God. We often turn to the worldly things surrounding us for gratification, only to find more calloused worldliness.

How much more beautiful the world will be when everyone hears and believes; when self-discipline prevails; and we are able to take pride in our actions. Then, love for all, God's gifts will be the way of life.

As we patiently wait for everyone to come into this fold, you and I, as Companions on Life's Journey with God, can listen to His gentle voice and enjoy a lifetime of peace... even in the midst of troubles.

The cross that greets pilgrims trekking to the of Cross Mountain, where Mary First Appeared to the Children in Medjugorje

EPILOGUE

As I share these stories of my life's journey, I recall so many more that I haven't shared. They do, however, remain in my mind and heart and I give thanks to God for every one of them. I never had big plans on how to spend the "Winter" years of my life; but now that they are here, I will enjoy the journey with a stronger acknowledgement and appreciation of God's companionship as he wraps his arms around me and leads me.

Now the book is done; so…what's next?

I do plan to continue spending some evening time playing the piano. This is very relaxing before bedtime. I never did learn how to play "The Flight of the Bumblebee." If I make this a life goal, I should be able to hang on until at least my 104th birthday! Maybe my sister, Marion can divinely help me achieve it sooner.

I will continue to quilt but not king-size quilts that I may not be able to finish. Instead, I think it will be cool to use all of the leftover fabric I have accumulated from all my previous projects and make table runners for family and friends.

I will continue to play bridge with friends. I have not put my paints aside yet. There is one more scene of the Rockies I would like to paint or maybe one last painting of a beautiful snow-covered Minnesota winter. And last, but not least, I will continue to praise the Lord with music on the piano and/or organ at St. Joe's as long as the good Lord allows!

I am looking forward, with excitement and anticipation, to the next chapter of my life whether it be tomorrow or ten years from now, because "Soon And Very Soon," I am going to see my Lord and all of my loved ones waiting for me to "Come Home" to "The City of God."

A painting I completed in 2021 for my grandson and his new wife.

This is a photo of my late son-in-law with the Rocky Mountains in the background.
Recreating it into a painting will be a joy.

Mary Garden at our little cabin in the woods.
Recreating this into a painting will be a joy and beautiful
reminder of my husband's deep devotion to Mary.

ACKNOWLEDGEMENTS

One more miracle is the completion of this book which wouldn't have been possible without all the support and love of my family.

- My daughter, Sue Lamour who has inherited her father's and grandfather's love for writing and prose; often offering positive views in challenging situations. Suesie has painstakingly edited and co-authored this book from cover to cover including the layout and design.

- My son, Mike who has been my rock.

  Mike is the first to call me in the morning to "check-in." Since the passing his father, Mike has lovingly taken over as guardian of the family and the caretaker of Jim's and my beloved cabin.

  Mike is humble with a giftedly mechanical mind that puts him in high demand to troubleshoot mechanical issues in a low-resource world – "up north." Many have seriously referenced Mike as "MacGyver." I looked up "MacGyver" recently in the Oxford dictionary. It didn't surprise me one bit to read: **Mac·Gy·ver:** *To make or repair (an object) in an improvised or inventive way, making use of whatever items are at hand.*

- My son, Dave: Better known as "Stump" to all - except his mother who insists on calling him by his given name.

  Dave is the one to check-in at the end of the day to see how it went. Dave, similar to Mike, is giftedly creative and always there to "fix" or "make" anything my heart desires whether he thinks it's necessary or not. He is a kind man with a kind heart who doesn't hesitate to "wear another man's shoes" in order to understand where they are coming from.

- My wonderful daughters-in-law, Nancy and Carole, who treat me like their own mother in all ways and will drop anything to come when I call. I couldn't live where I am without their help. Both are busy with their own lives and grandchildren but **always** have time for me and **never** make me feel like a burden.

- My daughter, Sharon, beautifully rounds out "Our Circle."

  Sharon is my "medical" caretaker, always ready to re-arrange whatever she is doing and fly or drive home to take care of my needs. She spent many days and nights with me when Jim was hospitalized; and on several occasions, when I was ill, she restructured her environment to just be present with me even when she, herself, was grieving. Sharon lost her husband to a terrible neurological disease a year after her dad died.

  Since Sharon's move to Colorado, it's not so easy to just hop in the car and go visit. But she makes it a point to call every day and welcomes my call, at literally **any** time, to just talk.

I love all my children dearly and remember the nights we would tuck them into bed after saying their prayers with their dad. Sleep well my dear children. God and your Guardian Angels are watching over you.

My children L-R: David (Stump), Sharon, Myself, Mike, Suesie

My children are not the only people who have gifted my life. I am grateful to have so many, I seriously don't know how to begin – or end my list. I will begin with:

- Mary Joe was one of the first people to befriend me when Jim and I moved to Grand Rapids. As we worked together in the fair both, I admired her for her contagious laugh and sense of humor. Even more, I admired her beautiful gift of awareness for those who need lifting up, even when she, herself, could use a lift. I look forward to laughing with you again in heaven, my dear friend.

- Our present pastor, Father Blake Rosier has been like a loving, caring grandson to me. He is a wonderful young priest who has so much responsibility for such a young priest. He is doing an awesome job and is loved by all.

- All the clergy Jim and I have been privileged to travel with on our journeys.
- My newest friend, Sarah who has taken on the job of music director at St. Joe's.

  Sarah accepts me where I am at and allows me to continue with my ministry as long as I am able.

- Ann, the music teacher at St. Joe's school who, like Sarah, allows me to "help" with whatever I wish at school. It's hard to let go of a job I truly loved and Ann so kindly accommodates me. I have worked with many teachers in my 30$^+$ years of teaching and Ann is the best of the best. It has been an honor to observe her teaching methods. God has blessed me with her friendship in my life's "winter" years.

- All of the members of St. Joe's choir, past and present. I will always have a warm spot in my heart for them.

- o Special mention goes to my tenor buddies, Corrine and Carol, who I have so enjoyed singing with for many years.

     Carol has taken on an additional role as my, "Nurse Nancy," accompanying me to Dr. appointments and explaining what I don't understand.
- o Two more tenors, Randy and Marv are no exception to what a gift this group is in my life.
- o Connie, Bobbie, and Bonnie and my new Cello friends have added so much to the choir because they are all so faithful and dependable.
- o Tom is unforgettable with his beautiful perfect pitch bass voice. He is a gift from God to our choir and our church community and is a true example of gifts from God helping us to experience and appreciate the beautiful colors and harmony those with special needs can bring to our lives.

- Marcie, my oldest friend (well, not "oldest," per say, but longest-running), was my husband's secretary and my go-to for just about everything. Marcie is funny, mischievous and a deeply spiritual confidant all rolled up in one bubbly giggling package. She pushed me beyond my boundaries and opened my mind to see different aspects of people and situations. Marcy and I have not had as much interaction since retirement and moving to different locations; but the bond we built is deeply rooted in my life and will never die. I miss you, my friend.

I don't know how to end my list. My life is so full. I pray that all who have touched my life, whether you are listed or not, know how grateful I am to you all for being companions on my life's journey with God.

Made in the USA
Monee, IL
24 January 2023

26056335R00056